A TALE OF THREE KINGS

BOOKS BY GENE EDWARDS

First-Century Diaries

The Silas Diary
The Titus Diary
The Timothy Diary
The Priscilla Diary
The Gaius Diary

An Introduction to the Deeper Christian Life

Living by the Highest Life
The Secret to the Christian Life
The Inward Journey

The Chronicles of Heaven

The Beginning
The Birth
The Escape
The Triumph
The Return

Healing for the Inner Man

Exquisite Agony
A Tale of Three Kings
The Prisoner in the Third Cell
Letters to a Devastated Christian
Dear Lillian

In a Class by Itself

The Divine Romance

Radical Books

Revolution: The Story of the Early Church
How to Meet in Homes
The Christian Woman . . . Set Free
Beyond Radical
Climb the Highest Mountain

Other Books

Christ Before Creation
One Hundred Days in the Secret Place
The Day I Was Crucified as Told by Jesus the Christ
Your Lord is a Blue Collar Worker

A TALE OF THREE KINGS

by

Gene Edwards

TYNDALE HOUSE PUBLISHERS, INC.
CAROL STREAM, ILLINOIS

Visit Tyndale's exciting Web site at www.tyndale.com.

TYNDALE and Tyndale's quill logo are registered trademarks of Tyndale House Publishers, Inc.

A Tale of Three Kings

Copyright © 1980, 1992 by Gene Edwards. All rights reserved.

Designed by Erik M. Peterson

Cover photograph copyright © by Dan Eckert/iStockphoto. All rights reserved.

This book was formerly published by SeedSowers (Christian Books Publishing House), Newnan, Georgia 30263.

Scripture quotations are taken from the *Holy Bible,* King James Version.

Printed in the United States of America

ISBN 978- 0-8423-6908-4

15   14   13   12   11   10
31   30   29   28   27   26

DEDICATION

*To the brokenhearted Christians
coming out of authoritarian groups, seeking solace,
healing, and hope. May you somehow recover
and go on with him who is liberty.*

*And to all brokenhearted Christians:
May you be so utterly healed that you can still answer
the call of him who asks for all because he is all.*

ACKNOWLEDGMENTS

To Helen, Carman, and Patty for aiding in the preparation of this manuscript.

Preface to the Second Edition

WHEN I FIRST PENNED *A Tale of Three Kings,* I would have been encouraged to know it would live long enough to go through two or three printings. I utterly underestimated the number of devastated Christians out there. A far broader audience than I anticipated has taken up this book. It is an audience made up of Christians damaged by such things as church splits and individual "Christian to Christian" clashes.

I have been a little awed by the reception of this book and the fact that the reception has been worldwide. The number of Christian workers who have ordered this book in bulk, to be passed out to their people, has been only short of phenomenal. That *A Tale of Three Kings* has been turned into plays and has been read publicly from pulpits turned awe to amazement.

Obviously, there is a great deal of pain and hurt out there in

Christendom that is rarely addressed or ministered to. I hope this book, as well as *Letters to a Devastated Christian, Crucified by Christians,* and *The Prisoner in the Third Cell,* will minister to those needs.

Author's Preface

WHY THIS BOOK AND WHAT IS ITS PURPOSE? The answer can probably be traced to my mailbox. As one who receives correspondence from Christians all over the world, I noted some years ago a growing number of letters from Christians devastated by the authoritarian movement that had become so popular with many evangelical groups. A reaction to this totalitarian concept eventually set in. A mass exodus was soon under way. The stories being told by these spiritual fugitives are often terrifying and sometimes unbelievable. I am not at all sure if it is the doctrine itself that is causing such widespread carnage or the inordinate practice of this doctrine. Whatever it is, in all my long years as an evangelical Christian minister, I have never seen anything that has damaged so many believers so deeply. The wreckage appears to be universal, and recovery from it is almost nil.

This book reflects my concern for this multitude of confused, brokenhearted, and often bitter Christians who now find their spiritual lives in shambles and who are groping about for even the slightest word of hope and comfort.

This book, I trust, will serve in some small way to meet this need.

There is one thing, dear reader, this book is most certainly not intended to be. It is not intended to be additional fodder in your cannon to better blast your adversaries, whatever your view. I would beg you to be done with such ancient and brutish ways. This book is intended for individual healing and for private retreat.

I trust this volume will sound a note of hope, even if that note is heard ever so distantly.

Gene Edwards

They have set up kings,
but not by me:
they have made princes,
and I knew it not . . .

HOSEA 8:4

Well, dear reader, how nice to be with you once more. It is a privilege to spend this time with you. Thank you for meeting here, and I suggest we hasten into the playhouse, as I see that they have already dimmed the lights.

There are two seats reserved for us not too far from the stage. Quickly, let us take them.

I understand the story is a drama. I trust, though, you will not find it sad.

I believe we will find the story to be in two parts. In part 1 we shall meet an older king, Saul by name, and a young shepherd boy named David. In part 2 we shall once more meet an older king and a young man. But this time the older king is David and the young man is Absalom.

The story is a portrait (you might prefer to call it a rough charcoal sketch) of submission and authority within the kingdom of God.

Ah, they have turned off the lights, and the players have taken their places. The audience has quieted itself. The curtain is rising.

Our story has begun.

Prologue

THE ALMIGHTY, living God turned to Gabriel and gave a command.

"Go, take these two portions of my being. There are two destinies waiting. To each unborn destiny give one portion of myself."

Carrying two glowing, pulsating lights of Life, Gabriel opened the door into the realm between two universes and disappeared. He had stepped into the Mall of Unborn Destinies.

Gabriel spoke: "I have here two portions of the nature of God. The first is the very cloth of his nature. When wrapped about you, it clothes you with the breath of God. As water surrounds a person in the sea, so will his very breath envelop you. With this, *the divine breath,* you will have his power—power to subdue armies, shame the enemies of God, and accomplish his work on the earth. Here is the power of God as a gift. Here is immersion into the Spirit."

A destiny stepped forward: "This portion of God is for me."

"True," replied the angel. "And remember, whoever receives such a great portion of power will surely be known by many. Ere your earthly pilgrimage is done, your true character will be known; yea, it will be *revealed* by means of this power. Such is the destiny of all who want and wield this portion, for it touches only the outer person, affecting the inner person not one whit. Outer power will always unveil the inner resources or the lack thereof."

The first destined one received the gift and stepped back.

Gabriel spoke again.

"I have here the second of two elements of the living God. This is not a gift but an inheritance. A gift is worn on the outer person; an inheritance is planted deep inside—like a seed. Yet, even though it is such a small planting, this planting grows and, in time, fills all the inner person."

Another destiny stepped forward. "I believe this element is to be mine for my earthly pilgrimage."

"True," responded the angel again. "I must tell you that what has been given to you is a glorious thing—the only element in the universe that can change the human heart. Yet even this element of God cannot accomplish its task nor grow and fill your entire inner being unless it is compounded well. It must be mixed lavishly with pain, sorrow, and crushing."

The second destined one received the inheritance and stepped back.

Beside Gabriel sat the angel Recorder. He dutifully entered into his ledger the record of the two destinies.

"And who shall these destinies become after they go through the door to the visible universe?" asked Recorder.

Gabriel replied softly, "Each, in his time, shall be king."

PART 1

Chapter 1

THE YOUNGEST SON of any family bears two distinctions: He is considered to be both spoiled and uninformed. Usually little is expected of him. Inevitably, he displays fewer characteristics of leadership than the other children in the family. As a child, he never leads. He only follows, for he has no one younger on whom to practice leadership.

So it is today. And so it was three thousand years ago in a village called Bethlehem, in a family of eight boys. The first seven sons of Jesse worked near their father's farm. The youngest was sent on treks into the mountains to graze the family's small flock of sheep.

On those pastoral jaunts, this youngest son always carried two things: a sling and a small, guitarlike instrument. Spare time for a sheepherder is abundant on rich mountain plateaus where sheep can graze for days in one sequestered meadow. But as time passed and days became weeks, the young man became very lonely. The feeling of friendlessness that always roamed inside him was magnified. He often cried. He also played his harp a great deal. He had a good voice, so he often sang. When these activities failed to comfort him, he gathered up a pile of stones and, one by one, swung them at a distant tree with something akin to fury.

When one rock pile was depleted, he would walk to the blistered tree, reassemble his rocks, and designate another leafy enemy at yet a farther distance.

He engaged in many such solitary battles.

This shepherd-singer-slinger also loved his Lord. At night, when all the sheep lay sleeping and he sat staring at the dying fire, he would strum upon his harp and break into quiet song. He sang the ancient hymns of his forefathers' faith. While he sang he wept, and while weeping he often broke out in abandoned praise—until mountains in distant places lifted up his praise and tears and passed them on to higher mountains, until they eventually reached the ears of God.

When the young shepherd did not praise and when he did not cry, he tended to each and every sheep and lamb. When not occupied with his flock, he swung his companionable sling and swung it again and again until he could tell every rock precisely where to go.

Once, while singing his lungs out to God, angels, sheep, and passing clouds, he spied a living enemy: a huge bear! He lunged forward. Both found themselves moving furiously toward the same small object, a lamb feeding at a table of rich, green grass. Youth and bear stopped halfway and whirled to face one another. Even as he instinctively reached into his pocket for a stone, the young man realized, "Why, I am not afraid."

Meanwhile, brown lightning on mighty, furry legs charged at the shepherd with foaming madness. Impelled by the strength of youth, the young man married rock to leather, and soon a brook-smooth pebble whined through the air to meet that charge.

A few moments later, the man—not quite so young as a moment before—picked up the little lamb and said, "I am your shepherd, and God is mine."

And so, long into the night, he wove the day's saga into a song. He hurled that hymn to the skies again and again until he had taught the melody and words to every angel that had ears. They, in turn, became custodians of this wondrous song and passed it on as healing balm to brokenhearted men and women in every age to come.

Chapter 2

A FIGURE IN THE DISTANCE was running toward him. It grew and became his brother. "Run!" cried the brother. "Run with all your strength. I'll watch the flock."

"Why?"

"An old man, a sage. He wants to meet all eight of the sons of Jesse, and he has seen all but you."

"But why?"

"Run!"

So David ran. He stopped long enough to get his breath. Then, sweat pouring down his sunburned cheeks, his red face matching his red curly hair, he walked into his father's house, his eyes recording everything in sight.

The youngest son of Jesse stood there, tall and strong, but more in the eyes of the curious old gentleman than to anyone else in the room. Kith and kin cannot always tell when a man is grown, even when looking straight at him. The elderly man saw. And something more he saw. In a way he himself did not understand, the old man knew what God knew.

God had taken a house-to-house survey of the whole kingdom in search of someone very special. As a result of this survey, the Lord God Almighty had found that this leather-lunged troubadour loved his Lord with a purer heart than anyone else on all the sacred soil of Israel.

"Kneel," said the bearded one with the long, gray hair. Almost regally, for one who had never been in that particular position, David knelt and then felt oil pouring down on his head. Somewhere, in one of the closets of his mind labeled "childhood information," he found a thought: *This is what men do to designate royalty! Samuel is making me a . . . what?*

The Hebrew words were unmistakable. Even children knew them.

"Behold the Lord's anointed!"

Quite a day for that young man, wouldn't you say? Then do you find it strange that this remarkable event led the young man not to the throne but to a decade of hellish agony and suffering? On that day, David was enrolled, not into the lineage of royalty but into the school of brokenness.

Samuel went home. The sons of Jesse, save one, went forth

to war. And the youngest, not yet ripe for war, received a promotion in his father's home . . . from sheepherder to messenger boy. His new job was to run food and messages to his brothers on the front lines. He did this regularly.

On one such visit to the battlefront, he killed another bear, in exactly the same way as he had the first. This bear, however, was nine feet tall and bore the name Goliath. As a result of this unusual feat, young David found himself a folk hero.

And eventually he found himself in the palace of a mad king. And in circumstances that were as insane as the king, the young man was to learn many indispensable lessons.

Chapter 3

DAVID SANG TO THE MAD KING. Often. The music helped the old man a great deal, it seems. And all over the palace, when David sang, everyone stopped in the corridors, turned their ears in the direction of the king's chamber, and listened and wondered. How did such a young man come to possess such wonderful words and music?

Everyone's favorite seemed to be the song the little lamb had taught him. They loved that song as much as did the angels.

Nonetheless, the king was mad, and therefore he was jealous. Or was it the other way around? Either way, Saul felt threatened by David, as kings often do when there is a popular, promising young man beneath them. The king also knew, as did David, that this boy just might have his job some day.

But would David ascend to the throne by fair means or foul?

Saul did not know. This question is one of the things that drove the king mad.

David was caught in a very uncomfortable position; however, he seemed to grasp a deep understanding of the unfolding drama in which he had been caught. He seemed to understand something that few of even the wisest men of his day understood. Something that in our day, when men are wiser still, even fewer understand.

And what was that?

God did not have—but wanted very much to have—men and women who would live in pain.

God wanted a broken vessel.

Chapter 4

THE MAD KING SAW DAVID as a threat to the *king's* kingdom. Saul did not understand, it seems, that God should be left to decide what kingdoms survive which threats. Not knowing this, Saul did what all mad kings do. He threw spears at David. He could. He was *king*. Kings can do things like that. They almost always do. Kings claim the right to throw spears. Everyone knows that kings have that right. Everyone knows very, very well. How do they know? Because the king has told them so—many, many times.

Is it possible that this mad king was the *true* king, even the Lord's anointed?

And what about your king? Is he the Lord's anointed? Maybe he is. Maybe he isn't. No one can ever really know for sure. Men say they are sure. Even *certain*. But they are not. They do not know. God knows. But he will not tell.

If your king is truly the Lord's anointed, and if he also *throws spears,* then there are some things you *can* know, and know for sure:

Your king is quite mad.

And he is a king after the order of King Saul.

Chapter 5

GOD HAS A UNIVERSITY. It's a small school. Few enroll; even fewer graduate. Very, very few indeed.

God has this school because he does not have broken men and women. Instead, he has several other types of people. He has people who claim to have God's authority . . . and don't—people who claim to be broken . . . and aren't. And people who *do have* God's authority, but who are mad *and* unbroken. And he has, regretfully, a great mixture of everything in between. All of these he has in abundance, but broken men and women, hardly at all.

In God's sacred school of submission and brokenness, why are there so few students? Because all students in this school must suffer much pain. And as you might guess, it is often the unbroken ruler (whom God sovereignly picks) who metes out the pain. David was once a student in this school, and Saul was God's chosen way to crush David.

As the king grew in madness, David grew in understanding. He knew that God had placed him in the king's palace under true authority.

The authority of King Saul was *true*? Yes, God's chosen authority. *Chosen for David.* Unbroken authority, yes. But divine in ordination, nonetheless.

Yes, that is possible.

David drew in his breath, placed himself under his mad king, and moved farther down the path of his earthly hell.

Chapter 6

DAVID HAD A QUESTION: What do you do when someone throws a spear at you?

Does it seem odd to you that David did not know the answer to this question? After all, everyone else in the world knows what to do when a spear is thrown at you. Why, you pick up the spear and throw it right back!

"When someone throws a spear at you, David, just wrench it out of the wall and throw it back. Everyone else does, you can be sure."

And in performing this small feat of returning thrown spears, you will prove many things: You are courageous. You stand for the right. You boldly stand against the wrong. You are tough and can't be pushed around. You will not stand for injustice or unfair treatment. You are the defender of the faith, keeper of the flame, detector of all heresy. You will not be wronged. All of these attributes then combine to prove that you are also a candidate for kingship. Yes, perhaps *you* are the Lord's anointed.

After the order of King Saul.

There is also a possibility that some twenty years after your coronation, you will be the most incredibly skilled spear thrower in all the realm. And also by then . . .

Quite mad.

Chapter 7

UNLIKE ANYONE ELSE in spear-throwing history, David did *not* know what to do when a spear was thrown at him. He did not throw Saul's spears back at him. Nor did he make any spears of his own and throw them. Something was different about David. All he did was dodge the spears.

What can a man, especially a young man, do when the king decides to use him for target practice? What if the young man decides not to return the compliment?

First of all, he must pretend he cannot see spears. Even when they are coming straight at him. Second, he must learn to duck very quickly. Last, he must pretend nothing happened.

You can easily tell when someone has been hit by a spear. He turns a deep shade of bitter. David never got hit. Gradually, he learned a very well-kept secret. He discovered three things that prevented him from ever being hit.

One, never learn anything about the fashionable, easily mastered art of spear throwing. Two, stay out of the company of all spear throwers. And three, keep your mouth tightly closed.

In this way, spears will never touch you, even when they pierce your heart.

Chapter 8

"My king is mad. At least, I so perceive him. What can I do?"

First, recognize this immutable fact: You cannot tell (none of us can) who is the Lord's anointed and who is not. Some kings, whom all agree are after the order of King Saul, are really after the order of David. And others, whom all agree are after the order of David, really belong to the order of King Saul. Who is correct? Who can know? To whose voice do you listen? *No man* is wise enough ever to break that riddle. All we can do is walk around asking ourselves this question:

"Is this man the Lord's anointed? And if he is, is he after the order of King Saul?"

Memorize that question very well. You may have to ask it of yourself ten thousand times. Especially if you are a citizen of a realm whose king just might be mad.

Asking this question may not seem difficult, but it is.

Especially when you are crying very hard . . . and dodging spears . . . and being tempted to throw one back . . . and being encouraged by others to do just that. And all your rationality and sanity and logic and intelligence and common sense agree. But in the midst of your tears and your frustration, remember that you know only the question, not the answer.

No one knows the answer.

Except God.

And he *never* tells.

Chapter 9

"I DID NOT LIKE THAT LAST CHAPTER. It skirted the problem. I'm in David's situation, and I am in agony. What do I do when the kingdom I'm in is ruled by a spear-wielding king? Should I leave? If so, how? Just what does a person *do* in the middle of a spear-throwing contest?"

Well, if you didn't like the *question* found in the last chapter, you won't like the *answer* found in this one.

The answer is "You get stabbed to death."

"But what is the good in being speared?"

You have your eyes on the wrong King Saul. As long as you look at your king, you will blame him, and him alone, for your present hell. But be careful, for God has *his* eyes fastened sharply on another King Saul. Not the visible one standing up there throwing spears at you. No, God is looking at *another* King Saul. One just as bad—or worse.

God is looking at the King Saul in *you*.

"In *me*?!"

Saul is in your bloodstream, in the marrow of your bones. He makes up the very flesh and muscle of your heart. He is mixed into your soul. He inhabits the nuclei of your atoms.

King Saul is one with you.

You are King Saul!

He breathes in the lungs and beats in the breast of all of us. There is only one way to get rid of him. He must be annihilated.

You may not find this to be a compliment, but at least now you know why God put you under someone who just might be King Saul.

David the sheepherder would have grown up to become King Saul II, except that God cut away the Saul inside David's heart. That operation, by the way, took years and was a brutalizing experience that almost killed the patient.

And what were the scalpel and tongs God used to remove this inner Saul? God used the outer Saul.

King Saul sought to destroy David, but his only success was that he became the instrument of God to put to death the Saul who roamed about in the caverns of David's own soul. Yes, David was virtually destroyed in the process, but this had to be. Otherwise the Saul in him would have survived.

David accepted this fate. He embraced the cruel circumstances. He lifted no hand nor offered resistance. Nor did he grandstand his piety. Silently, privately, he bore the crucible of humiliation. Because of this he was deeply wounded. His whole inner being was mutilated. His personality was altered. When the gore was over, David was barely recognizable.

You weren't satisfied with the question in the last chapter? Then you probably didn't like the answer in this one.

None of us do.

Except God.

Chapter 10

HOW DOES A PERSON KNOW when it is finally time to leave the Lord's anointed—especially if the Lord's anointed is after the order of King Saul?

David never made that decision. The Lord's anointed made it for him. The king's own decree settled the matter!

"Hunt him down; kill him like a dog."

Only then did David leave. No, he fled. Even then, he never spoke a word or lifted a hand against Saul. And please note this: David did not split the kingdom when he made his departure. He did not take part of the population with him. He left *alone*.

Alone. *All* alone. King Saul II never does that. He always takes those who "insist on coming along."

Yes, people do insist on going with you, don't they? They are willing to help you found the kingdom of King Saul II.

Such men *never* dare leave alone.

But David left alone. You see, the Lord's true anointed can leave alone.

There's only *one* way to leave a kingdom:

Alone.

All alone.

Chapter 11

CAVES ARE NOT THE IDEAL PLACE for morale building. There is a certain sameness to them all, no matter how many you have lived in. Dark. Wet. Cold. Stale. A cave becomes even worse when you are its sole inhabitant . . . and in the distance you can hear the dogs baying.

But sometimes, when the dogs and hunters were not near, the hunted sang. He started low, then lifted his voice and sang the song the little lamb had taught him. The cavern walls echoed each note just as the mountains had once done. The music rolled down into deep cavern darkness that soon became an echoing choir singing back to him.

He had less now than when he was a shepherd, for now he had no lyre, no sun, not even the company of sheep. The memories of the court had faded. David's greatest ambition now reached no higher than a shepherd's staff. *Everything* was being crushed out of him.

He sang a great deal.

And matched each note with a tear.

How strange, is it not, what suffering begets?

There in those caves, drowned in the sorrow of his song and in the song of his sorrow, David became the greatest hymn writer and the greatest comforter of broken hearts this world shall ever know.

Chapter 12

HE RAN—through soggy fields and down slimy riverbeds. Sometimes the dogs came close; sometimes they even *found* him. But swift feet, rivers, and watery pits hid him. He took his food from the fields, dug roots from the roadside, slept in trees, hid in ditches, crawled through briars and mud. For days he ran—not daring to stop or eat. He drank the rain. Half naked, all filthy, on he walked, stumbled, crawled, and clawed.

Caves were castles now. Pits were home.

In times past, mothers had always told their children that if they did not behave they would end up like the town drunk. No longer. They had a better, more frightening story. "Be good, or you'll end up like the giant killer."

In Jerusalem, when teachers taught students to be submissive to the king and to honor the Lord's anointed, David was the parable. "See, this is what God does to rebellious men." The young listeners shuddered at the thought and somberly resolved never to have anything to do with rebellion.

So it was then, so it is now, and so it shall ever be.

Much later, David would reach a foreign land and a small—very small—measure of safety. Here, too, he was feared, hated, lied about, and plotted against. He shook hands with murder on several occasions.

These were David's darkest hours. We know them as his pre-king days, but he didn't. He may have assumed this was his lot forever.

Suffering was giving birth. Humility was being born.

By earthly measures he was a shattered man; by heaven's measure, a broken one.

Chapter 13

OTHERS HAD TO FLEE as the king's madness grew. First one, then three, then ten, and eventually hundreds. After long searching, some of these fugitives made contact with David. They had not seen him for a long time.

The truth was that when they did see him, they didn't recognize him. He had changed. His personality, his disposition, his total being had been altered. He talked less. He loved God more. He sang differently. They had never heard these songs before. Some were lovely beyond words, but some could freeze the blood in your veins.

Those who found him and decided to be his fellow fugitives were a sorry, worthless lot: thieves, liars, complainers, faultfinders, rebellious men with rebellious hearts. They were blind with hate for the king and, therefore, for all authority figures.

They would have been troublemakers in paradise, if ever they could have gotten in.

David did not lead them. He did not share their attitudes. Yet, unsolicited, they began to follow him.

He never spoke to them of authority. He never spoke of submission. But every one of them submitted. He laid down no rules. *Legalism* is not a word found in the vocabulary of fugitives. Nonetheless, they cleaned up their outward lives. Gradually, their inward lives began to change, too.

They didn't fear submission or authority. They didn't even think about the topic, much less discuss it. Then why did they follow him? They didn't, exactly. It was just that he was . . . well . . . David. That didn't need explanation.

And so, for the first time, true kingship had its nativity.

Chapter 14

"WHY, DAVID, WHY?"

The place was another nameless cave.

The men stirred about restlessly. Gradually, and very uneasily, they began to settle in. All were as confused as Joab, who had finally voiced their questions.

Joab wanted some answers. Now!

David should have seemed embarrassed or at least defensive. He was neither. He was looking past Joab like a man viewing another realm that only he could see.

Joab walked directly in front of David, looked down on him, and began roaring his frustrations.

"Many times he almost speared you to death in his palace. I saw that with my own eyes. Finally, you ran away. Now for years you have been nothing but a rabbit for him to chase. Furthermore, the whole world believes the lies he tells about you. He has come—the king himself—hunting every cave, pit, and hole on earth to find you and kill you like a dog. But tonight *you* had *him* at the end of his own spear and you did nothing!

"Look at us. We're animals again. Less than an hour ago you could have freed us all. Yes, we could all be free, right now! Free! And Israel, too. She would be free. Why, David? Why did you not end these years of misery?"

There was a long silence. Men shifted again, uneasily. They were not accustomed to seeing David rebuked.

"Because," said David very slowly (and with a gentleness that seemed to say, I heard what you asked, but not the way you asked it), "because once, long ago, he was not mad. He was young. He was great. Great in the eyes of God and men. And it was God who made him king—God—not men."

Joab blazed back, "But now he is *mad*! And God is no longer with him. And David, he will yet kill you!"

This time it was David's answer that blazed with fire.

"Better he kill me than I learn his ways. Better he kill me than I become as he is. I shall not practice the ways that cause kings to go mad. I will not throw spears, nor will I allow hatred to grow in my heart. I will not avenge. I will not destroy the Lord's anointed. Not now. Not ever!"

Joab could not handle such a senseless answer. He stormed out into the dark.

That night men went to bed on cold, wet stone and muttered about their leader's distorted, masochistic views of relationships to kings—especially mad ones.

Angels went to bed that night, too, and dreamed, in the afterglow of that rare, rare day, that God might yet be able to give his authority to a trustworthy vessel.

Chapter 15

WHAT KIND OF MAN WAS SAUL? Who was this one who made himself David's enemy? Anointed of God. Deliverer of Israel. And yet remembered mostly for his madness.

Forget the bad press. Forget the stinging reviews. Forget his reputation. Look at the facts. Saul was one of the greatest figures of human history. He was a farm boy, a country kid who made good. He was tall, good-looking, and well-liked.

He was baptized into the Spirit of God.

He also came from a good family. In his lineage were some of the greatest historical figures of all humanity. Abraham, Jacob, Moses—these were his ancestors.

Do you remember the background? Abraham had founded a nation. Moses had set that nation free from slavery. Joshua gave those people a toehold in the land that God had promised them. The judges kept the whole thing from disintegrating into total chaos. That's when Saul came along. It was Saul who took these people and welded them into a united kingdom.

Saul united a people and founded a kingdom. Few men have ever done that. He created an army out of thin air. He won battles in the power of God, defeated the enemy again and again, as few men have ever done. Remember that, and remember that this man was immersed in the Spirit. Furthermore, he was a prophet. The Spirit came on him in power and authority. He did and said unprecedented things, and it was all by the power of the Spirit resting on him.

He was everything people today are seeking to be . . . empowered with the Holy Spirit . . . able to do the impossible . . . for God. A leader, chosen by God with power from God.

Saul was given authority that is God's alone. He was God's anointed, and God treated him that way.

He was also eaten with jealousy, filled with self-importance, and willing to live in spiritual darkness.

Is there a moral in these contradictions? Yes, and it will splinter a lot of your concepts about power, about great men and women under God's anointing, and about God himself.

Many pray for the power of God. More every year. Those prayers sound powerful, sincere, godly, and without ulterior motive. Hidden under such prayer and fervor, however, are ambition, a craving for fame, the desire to be considered a spiritual giant. The person who prays such a prayer may not even know it, but dark motives and desires are in his heart . . . in *your* heart.

Even as people pray these prayers, they are hollow inside. There is little internal spiritual growth. Prayer for power is the quick and the short way, circumnavigating internal growth.

There is a vast difference between the outward clothing of the Spirit's power and the inward filling of the Spirit's life. In the first, despite the power, the hidden man of the heart may remain unchanged. In the latter, that monster is dealt with.

Interesting about God. He hears all those requests for power, which fervent young men and women pray (in every generation), and he answers them! Very often he grants these requests for power, for authority. Sometimes, in answering them, he says yes to some very unworthy vessels.

He gives unworthy people his power? Even though they are a pile of dead men's bones inside?

Why does God do such a thing? The answer is both simple and shocking. He sometimes gives unworthy vessels a greater portion of power so that others will eventually see the *true* state of internal nakedness within that individual.

So think again when you hear the power merchant. Remember, God sometimes gives power to people for unseen reasons. A person can be living in the grossest of sin, and the outer gift will still be working perfectly. The gifts of God, once given, cannot be recalled. Even in the presence of sin. Furthermore, some people, living just such lives, *are* the Lord's anointed . . . in the Lord's eyes. Saul was living proof of this fact.

The gifts cannot be revoked. Terrifying, isn't it?

If you are young and have never seen such things, you may be certain that sometime in the next forty years you will see. Highly gifted and very powerful men and women . . . reputed to be leaders in the kingdom of God, do some very dark and ugly deeds.

What does this world need: gifted men and women, outwardly empowered? Or individuals who are broken, inwardly transformed?

Keep in mind that some who have been given the very power of God have raised armies, defeated the enemy, brought forth mighty works of God, preached and prophesied with unparalleled power and eloquence . . .

And thrown spears,

And hated other people,

And attacked others,

And plotted to kill,

And prophesied naked,

And even consulted witches.

Chapter 16

"YOU STILL HAVEN'T ANSWERED my question. The man I sit under: I think he is a King Saul. How can I know with certainty?"

It is not given to us to know. And remember, even Sauls are often the Lord's anointed.

You see, there are always people—everywhere, in every age, and in every group—who will stand and tell you: "That man is after the order of King Saul." While another, just as sure, will rise to declare, "No, he is the Lord's anointed after the order of David." No one can *really* know which of the two is correct. And if you happen to be in the balcony looking down at those men screaming at one another, you may wonder to which order *they* belong.

Remember, your leader may be a David.

"That's impossible!"

Is it? Most of us know at least two men in the lineage of David who have been damned and crucified by other men. By men who were absolutely certain the ones they were crucifying were *not* Davids.

And if you don't know of two such cases, for sure you know of one.

Men who go after the Sauls among us often crucify the Davids among us.

Who, then, can know who is a David and who is a Saul?

God knows. But he won't tell.

Are you so certain your king is a Saul and not a David that you are willing to take the position of God and go to war against your Saul? If so, then thank God you did not live in the days of crucifixion.

What, then, can you do? Very little. Perhaps nothing.

However, the passing of time (and the behavior of your leader while that time passes) reveals a great deal about your leader.

And the passing of time, and the way you react to that leader—be he David or Saul—reveals a great deal about *you*.

Chapter 17

TWO GENERATIONS AFTER THE REIGN OF SAUL, a young man enthusiastically enrolled himself into the ranks of Israel's army under a new king, the grandson of David. He soon began hearing tales of David's mighty men of valor. He set out to discover if one of those mighty men might still be alive and, if so, to find him and talk to him, though he calculated that such a man would be over a hundred years in age.

At last he discovered that, sure enough, one such man still lived. Having learned of his whereabouts, the youth hastened to his dwelling. Anxiously, if not hesitantly, he knocked on the door. Slowly it opened. There stood a giant of a man, gray . . . no, white haired . . . and wrinkled beyond expectation.

"Are you, sir, one of David's mighty men of long ago—one of those men of whom we have heard so much?"

For a long moment the old man surveyed the young man's

face, his features, his uniform. Then, in an ancient but firm voice, he replied, never taking his steady gaze off the young man's face.

"If you are asking if I am a former thief and cave dweller and one who followed a sobbing, hysterical fugitive, then yes, I was one of the 'mighty men of David.'"

He straightened his shoulders with those last words. Nonetheless, his sentence ended in a chuckle.

"But, sir, you make the great king sound like a weakling. Was he not the greatest of all rulers?"

"He was no weakling," said the old man. Then sizing up the motivation for the eager young man's presence at his door, he replied wisely and softly, "Nor was he a great leader."

"Then what, good sir? For I have come to learn the ways of the great king and his . . . uh . . . mighty men. What *was* the greatness of David?"

"I see you have the ambitions typical of youth," said the old warrior. "I have the distinct notion you dream of leading men yourself one day." He paused, then continued reflectively. "Yes, I'll tell you of the greatness of my king, but my words may surprise you."

The old man's eyes filled with tears as he thought first of David and then of the foolish new king only recently crowned.

"I will tell you of my king and his greatness: My king never threatened me as yours does. Your new king has begun his reign with laws, rules, regulations, and fear. The clearest memory I have of my king, when we lived in the caves, is that his was a life of *submission*. Yes, David showed me submission, not authority. He taught me not the quick cure of rules and laws, but the art of patience. *That* is what changed my life. Legalism is nothing but a leader's way of avoiding suffering.

"Rules were invented by elders so they could get to bed early! Men who speak endlessly on authority only prove they have none. And kings who make speeches about submission only betray twin fears in their hearts: They are not certain they are really true leaders, sent of God. And they live in mortal fear of a rebellion.

"My king spoke not of submitting to him. He feared no rebellion . . . because he did not mind if he was dethroned!

"David taught me losing, not winning. Giving, not taking. He showed me that the leader, not the follower, is inconvenienced. David shielded us from suffering; he did not mete it out.

"He taught me that authority yields to rebellion, especially when that rebellion is nothing more dangerous than immaturity, or perhaps stupidity." The old man was obviously remembering some very tense and perhaps humorous episodes in the caves.

"No," he said, now in a voice with a touch of eloquence, "authority from God is not afraid of challengers, makes no defense, and cares not one whit if it must be dethroned.

"That was the greatness of the great . . . of the *true* king."

The old man began to walk away. Both anger and regal patience were evident in his bearing as he turned. Then he faced the youth once more, thundering one last salvo: "As far as David's having authority: Men who don't have it talk about it all the time. Submit, submit! That's all you hear. David had authority, but I don't think that fact ever occurred to him. We were six hundred no-goods with a leader who cried a lot. That's all we were!"

Those were the last words the young soldier heard from the old warrior. Slipping back into the street, he wondered if he would ever again be happy serving under Rehoboam.

Chapter 18

So, HAVING COME TO THE END of our study of Saul and David, do you feel greatly assisted? What's that? You are now certain the man you are under is not truly from God . . . or if he is, he is at best only a Saul? My, how certain we mortals can be . . . of things even angels do not know.

May I ask you then, what you plan to do with this newly acquired knowledge? Yes, I am aware that you yourself are neither a Saul nor a David . . . but only a peasant of the realm. You do plan, though, to share your new discoveries with a few friends? I see. Then perhaps I should warn you that there is great danger with this heady new knowledge of yours. A strange mutation can take place within your own heart. You see, it is possible . . . but wait!

What is it I see over there? There . . . in that distant mist behind you. Turn. Do you see? Who is that figure making his way through the fog? It seems I have surely seen him before.

Look closely. Is it not possible for us to make out what he is doing?

He appears to be bending over some ancient chest. Yes, he has opened it.

Who is he? And what is he doing?

He has taken something out of the chest. A cloak? It is some kind of cape. Why, he is putting it on! The thing fits him perfectly, falling about his shoulders like a mantle.

Now what? He reaches again into that chest. I know I have seen that person somewhere before. What is it he pulls forth this time? A shield? No, a coat of arms. Yes, a coat of arms from some ancient, long-forgotten order. He holds it up as one who would make that order his own! Who is that man? The bearing. The stance. The carriage. I've seen it before. I'm sure.

Ah! He has moved out of the mist into the light. We will see him clearly now.

That face. Is it not you?!

Yes. It is. It is *you*! You who can so wisely discern the presence of an unworthy Saul!

Go! Look in yon mirror. That man is *you*! Look, too, at the name upon that coat of arms.

Behold: Absalom the Second!

PART 2

Chapter 19

"LOOK! HERE COMES DAVID!"

Bright smiles, a few giggles, some light laughter.

"See! It's David, no less."

Again, wide grins, a wave, and quiet amusement.

"That isn't King David," exclaimed a youth to his guardian as the two walked along the side of the street. "Why do they speak that way? That man is not David!"

"True, child, it is not David. It's only Absalom coming from the gate."

"Why do they call him David?" the boy asked, looking back over his shoulder at the handsome man in the chariot with the fifty men running before him.

"Because he reminds us all of David when he was young. And because we are all so glad that such a fine young man will take David's place someday. And perhaps, too, because Absalom is even better looking than David. He may be the most handsome man alive."

"Will Absalom be king soon? How old is King David, anyway? Is he about to die?"

"Of course not, my boy. Let's see . . . how old is David? Probably about the same age as King Saul when his reign came to an end."

"How old is Absalom?"

"About the same age as David when Saul was trying so hard to kill him."

"David is Saul's age. Absalom is the age of David when he first became king," mused the boy. They walked on silently for a while. The boy, obviously deep in thought, spoke again.

"Saul was very hard on David, was he not?"

"Yes, very."

"Is King David going to treat Absalom the same way Saul treated David? Will David be hard on Absalom?"

The guardian paused to consider the question, but the child went on: "If David treats Absalom badly, will Absalom behave with as much grace as David did?"

"Child, the future will surely tell us. My, you ask such questions! If, when you are grown, you can give answers as well as you now ask questions, you will surely be known as the wisest man on earth."

The two turned in at the palace gate.

Chapter 20

IT WARMED YOUR HEART to know a man who saw things so clearly. Discerning. Yes, that was the word that best described Absalom—*discerning*. He could penetrate to the heart of any problem.

Men felt secure just being with him. They even longed to have time with him. Talking with him, they realized that they themselves were wiser than they realized. Such a revelation made them feel good. As he discussed problem after problem and solution after solution, men began to long for the day when this one would be their leader. He could right so many wrongs. He gave them a sense of hope.

But this imposing, insightful man would never deliberately hasten the day of his own rule. They were confident of that. He was far too humble, too respectful of his father. And those around him began to feel a little frustrated that they would have to keep waiting for the better days of this man's rule.

The more they sat in his living room and talked, the more they realized that things were amiss in the kingdom. Yes, things amiss that they had never thought of before. And problems. Problems were coming to light of which they had never dreamed. Yes, they really were growing in wisdom and insight.

As the days passed, more and more of them came to listen. Word spread quietly. "Here is one who understands and has the answers." The frustrated came. They listened. They asked questions. They received excellent answers and began to hope.

Heads nodded. Dreams were born. As time passed, there were more such gatherings. Ideas turned into stories, stories of injustice that others might have deemed trivial. But not this listener! He was compassionate. And as those around him talked, the discovered injustices seemed to grow in number and severity. With each new story, men were more shocked at unfairness that was now, it seemed, rampant.

But the wise young man sat quietly and added not a word to these murmurings. He was too noble, you see. He always closed the evening conversations with a humble word of deference toward those in positions of responsibility. . . .

But it was too much to expect that any man could sit quietly by forever. This endless parade of injustice was bound to stir even the most respectful man. Even the purest in heart would be smitten with anger. (And this man was certainly the very purest in heart!)

Such a compassionate man could not forever turn his face from these sufferings nor forever remain silent. Such a noble character as this had to speak out someday.

Finally, his followers, which he vowed he did not have, were almost livid. Their insights into the wrongdoings of the kingdom not only grew but abounded. They all wanted to do something about these endless injustices.

At last, it seemed, the magnificent young man might concede. At the outset it was only a word. Later, a sentence. Men's hearts leaped. Joy, if not glee, reigned. Nobility was at last being aroused to action. But no! He cautioned them not to misunderstand. He was grieved, yes, but he could not speak against those in seats of responsibility. No, absolutely not. No matter how great the grievances, no matter how justified the frustration. He would not.

Yet he grieved more and more. It was obvious that some reports drove him to agony. Finally, his righteous anger broke out in cool, controlled words of strength. "These things ought not to be." He stood, eyes blazing. "If I were in responsibility, this is what I would do. . . ."

And with these words, the rebellion was ignited. Ignited in all but one, that is. In the man who seemed noblest and purest, this was not the case.

Rebellion had been in his heart for years.

Chapter 21

"SAGE!"

"Yes?"

"Sage, may I have a moment of your time?"

"Why, of course. I have a great deal of time."

"You have just come from a gathering of friends at Absalom's home?"

"Yes, that is correct."

"Would you mind sharing some of the impressions you had while there?"

"You mean a general impression of Absalom and his friends?"

"Yes, that would be good enough."

"Well, I have met many men like Absalom. Many."

"Then what is he like?"

"He is both sincere and ambitious. A contradiction, perhaps, but true, nonetheless. He probably means some of what he says. But his ambition will continue long after he discovers his inability to do the things he promises. Righting the wrongs always becomes secondary to ascent to power."

"I'm sorry, Sage, I do not understand."

"Two things stand out in my mind. At one gathering, when Absalom was answering questions, he was very emphatic that there should be more freedom in the kingdom. Everyone liked that. 'A people should be led only by God and not by men,' he said. 'Men should do only what they feel led of God to do. We should follow God, not a man.' I believe those were his words.

"At another meeting he spoke of the great visions he had for God's kingdom—of the great achievements the people were capable of. On the other hand, he spoke of many changes he would make in the way the kingdom is run. Although he did not seem to notice it, he had stated two irreconcilable propositions: many changes, more freedom.

"Yes, indeed, he does remind me of many other men I have encountered over the passing years."

"Sage, I think I understand what you've said, but I'm not sure what your point is."

"Absalom dreams. Dreams of what should be, of what *will*

be: 'This is what *I* will do,' he says. But to fulfill those dreams, he must have the people's cooperation. Ah, this is the point often overlooked. Such dreams rest totally on the premise that the people of God will follow the new leader, that *all* will see as he sees. Such men as Absalom can envision no problems in their own future kingdom. Possibly the people *will* follow, but possibly they will not.

"At most, the Lord's people will follow a leader for a few years. They never support anyone very long. Generally, people do what they please. They can be stopped to do someone else's pleasure for a time, but not for long. People will not work too hard, even if they are following *God.*

"What will Absalom do when people stop following *him* willingly? Ah, now there is a question.

"You see, there is no kingdom without discord. Even God had his critics in heaven, you know. All kingdoms follow a bumpy course. And people, especially God's people, never follow any dream in unison. No, to accomplish all he spoke of tonight will take time. Not all will be willing to go along. Will he still be determined to put all his dreams into being? If so, then Absalom has but one recourse: *dictatorship.* Either that, or he will see few, if any, of his grand dreams accomplished. And if he does become a dictator, I can assure you that soon there will be discontent with *him,* just as there is now with the present king. Yes, if Absalom becomes king, soon thereafter you will see new meetings like the one we have just come from tonight . . . only with new faces, new dreams, and plans for a new rebellion. And that gathering will be against Absalom! Then, when *Absalom* hears of such a meeting and of discussion about a rebellion, he will have but one recourse."

"What do you feel he will do, Sage?"

"Rebels who ascend to the throne by rebellion have no patience with other rebels and their rebellions. When Absalom is faced with rebellion, he will become a tyrant. He will bring ten times the evil he sees in your present king. He will squelch rebellion and rule with an iron hand . . . and by fear. He will eliminate all opposition. This is always the final stage of high-sounding rebellions. Such will be Absalom's way if he takes the throne from David."

"But, Sage, have not some rebellions been of benefit, throwing out brutes and despots?"

"Oh, yes, a few. But I remind you: This particular kingdom is different from all others. This kingdom is composed of God's people. It is a spiritual kingdom. I tell you emphatically, no rebellion in the kingdom of God is proper, nor can it ever be fully blessed."

"Why do you say this, Sage?"

"For many reasons. One is obvious. In the spiritual realm, those who lead rebellions have already proven, no matter how grandiose their words or angelic their ways, that they have a critical nature, an unprincipled character, and hidden motives in their hearts. Frankly, they are thieves. They create dissatisfaction and tension within the realm and then either seize power or siphon off followers. They use their followers to found their own dominions. Such a sorry beginning, built on the foundation of insurrection. . . . No, God never honors division in his realm.

"I find it curious that those who feel qualified to split God's kingdom do not feel capable of going somewhere else—to another land—to raise up a completely new kingdom. No, they must steal from another leader. I have never seen the exception. They seem always to need at least a few prepackaged followers.

"Beginning empty-handed and alone frightens the best of men. It also speaks volumes of just how sure they are that God is with them. Their every word, if truly understood, tells of their insecurity.

"There are many lands unspoiled and unpossessed. There are many people in other places waiting to follow a true king, a true man of God. Why don't 'would-be kings and prophets' simply walk quietly away, alone, then find another people in another place, and there raise up the kingdom they envision?

"Those who lead rebellions in the spiritual world are unworthy. There are no exceptions. And now I must go. I must join the passing parade."

"Tell me, Sage, what is your name?"

"My name? I am History."

Chapter 22

DAVID STOOD ON THE BALCONY overlooking the gardened terrace of his palace. The lights from the houses in the Holy City twinkled below him. From behind, a man approached. David sighed and, without turning, spoke. "Yes, Joab, what is it?"

"Have you heard?"

"Yes, I've heard," he replied quietly.

"How long have you known?" asked Joab with anxious surprise.

"For months, years, perhaps a decade. Perhaps I have known for thirty years."

Joab was not sure, after this answer, if they were speaking of the same subject. Absalom, after all, was not much past thirty. "Sir, I speak of Absalom," he said a little hesitantly.

"As do I," said the king.

"If you have known so long, why did you not stop him?"

"I was just asking myself that same question."

"Shall I stop him for you?"

David whirled round! In one instant, Joab's query had resolved his dilemma.

"No! Nor shall you speak one word to him. Nor shall you criticize him. Nor shall you allow anyone else to speak critically of him or what he is doing. Certainly you shall not stop him."

"But will he not then take the kingdom?"

David sighed again, softly, slowly. For a moment he balanced between tears and a smile. Then he smiled lightly and said, "Yes, perhaps he will."

"What will you do? Do you have plans?"

"No. None. Quite frankly, I have no idea what to do. I have fought many battles and faced many sieges. I have usually known what to do. But for this occasion, I have only the experience of my youth to draw on. The course I followed at that time seems to be the best I can follow now."

"And what course was that?"

"To do absolutely nothing."

Chapter 23

DAVID WAS ALONE AGAIN. Slowly, quietly, he walked the length of his rooftop garden. Finally he paused and spoke aloud to himself.

"I have waited, Absalom. I have waited and watched for years. I have asked again and again, 'What is in the heart of this young man?' And now I know. You will do the unthinkable. You will divide the very kingdom of God. All else was talk."

David was quiet for a moment. Then, almost in awe, he spoke, his voice hushed. "Absalom does not hesitate to divide the *kingdom of God.*

"Now I know. He seeks followers. Or at least he does not turn them away. Though he seems magnificently pure and noble, still he divides. His followers grow, even though he states convincingly that he has none."

For a long time David said nothing. Finally, with a trace of humor in his words, he began to address himself. "All right, good King David, you have one issue resolved. You are in the middle of a division, and you may very well be dethroned. Now, to the second issue." He paused, lifted his hand and, almost fatally, asked, "What will you *do*?

"The kingdom hangs in the balance. It seems I have two choices: to lose everything or to be a Saul. I can stop Absalom. I need only to be a Saul. In my old age, shall I now become a Saul? I feel the Lord himself awaits my decision.

"Shall I now be a Saul?" he asked himself again, this time loudly.

A voice from behind answered, "Good King, he has been no David to you."

David turned. It was Abishai who had approached unannounced.

"A crowded place, this terrace," quipped David.

"Sir?" said Abishai.

"Nothing. Suffice it to say I have not been without visitors today—a day when I would have chosen solitude. What did you say to me? In fact, what did I say?"

"You said, 'Shall I be a Saul to Absalom?' and I replied, 'He has been no young David to you.'"

"I never challenged Saul; I never attempted to divide the kingdom during his reign. Is that what you are saying?"

"More," replied Abishai strongly. "Saul was evil toward you and made your life torture. You responded only with respect and private agony. The bad things that happened in those days came only from one side. All fell on you. Yet you could have divided the kingdom and probably could have overthrown Saul. But rather than do that, you left the kingdom. You fled rather than cause division. You risked your life for unity and sealed your lips and eyes to all his injustices. You had more cause to rebel than any man in the history of this—or of any kingdom that has ever been. Absalom has to twist hard to conjure up his list of injustices . . . few of them significant, I might add.

"Has Absalom behaved as you did? Has Absalom respected you? Does Absalom seek to preserve the kingdom? Does he refuse to speak against you? Does Absalom turn aside followers? Has Absalom left the land to prevent its being sundered? Is Absalom respectful? Does he bear suffering in silent agony? Have bad things fallen on Absalom?

"No, he is only pure and noble!"

Abishai's last words came out almost in bites. Then he continued, more gravely this time.

"His grievances are minor compared to your rightful

grievances toward Saul. You never mistreated Saul. And you have never, in any way, been unfair to Absalom."

David interrupted with a grin. "I seem to have a gift for making old men and young men hate me without a cause. In my youth, the old attacked me; when I am old, the young attack me. What a marvelous achievement."

"My point," continued Abishai, "is that Absalom is no David. Therefore I ask you: Why don't you stop his rebellion? Stop him, the miserable . . ."

"Careful, Abishai. Remember he is also a son of the king. We should never speak ill of the son of a king."

"Good King, I remind you that you refused to raise your sword or your spear even once against Saul. But Absalom speaks against you night and day. He will one day—soon— raise an army against you. Nay, a nation. *This* nation! Young Absalom is no young David. I counsel you to stop him!"

"You are asking me, Abishai, to become a Saul," David replied heavily.

"No, I'm simply saying he is no David. Stop him!"

"And if I stop him, will I still be a David? If I stop him, will I not be a Saul?" asked the king, his eyes piercing Abishai. "To stop him, I must become either a Saul or an Absalom."

"My king and my friend, I speak to you fondly: I sometimes think you are a bit insane."

"Yes, I can see why," chuckled David.

"Dear King, Saul was a bad king. Absalom is, in some ways, a youthful incarnation of Saul. You alone are constant. You are forever the brokenhearted shepherd boy. Tell me truthfully, what do you plan?"

"Until now, I have not been sure. But of this I am certain: In my youth I was no Absalom. And in my old age I shall not be a Saul. In my youth, by your own words, I was David. In my old age I intend to be David still. Even if it costs me a throne, a kingdom, and perhaps my head."

Abishai said nothing for a while. Then, slowly, he spoke, making sure he grasped the significance of David's decision.

"You were not an Absalom, and you refuse to be a Saul. Sir, if you are not willing to put Absalom down, then I suggest we prepare to evacuate the kingdom. For Absalom will surely take the throne."

"Only as surely as King Saul killed the shepherd boy," replied the wise old king.

"What?" asked Abishai, startled.

"Think on it, Abishai. God once delivered a defenseless

shepherd boy from the powerful, mad king. He can yet deliver an old ruler from an ambitious young rebel."

"You underestimate your adversary," retorted Abishai.

"You underestimate my God," replied David serenely.

"But why, David? Why not fight?"

"I will give you the answer. And you will recall—for you were there—that I once gave this same answer to Joab in a cave long ago!

"It is better that I be defeated, even killed, than to learn the ways of . . . of a Saul or the ways of an Absalom. The kingdom is not that valuable. Let him have it, if that be the Lord's will. I repeat: I *shall not* learn the ways of either Saul or Absalom.

"And now, being an old man, I will add a word I might not have known then. Abishai, no man knows his own heart. I certainly do not know mine. Only God does. Shall I defend my little realm in the name of God? Shall I throw spears, and plot and divide . . . and kill men's spirits if not their bodies . . . to protect *my* empire? I did not lift a finger to be *made* king. Nor shall I do so to preserve a kingdom. Even the kingdom of God! God put me here. It is not my responsibility to take, or *keep*, authority. Do you not realize, it may be *his* will for these things to take place? If he chooses, God can protect and keep the kingdom even now. After all, it is *his* kingdom.

"As I said, no man knows his own heart. I do not know mine. Who knows what is really in my heart? Perhaps in God's eyes I am no longer worthy to rule. Perhaps he *is* through with me. Perhaps it is his will for Absalom to rule. I honestly don't know. And if this is his will, I want it. God may be finished with me!

"Any young rebel who raises his hand against a Saul, or any old king who raises his hand against an Absalom, may—in truth—be raising his hand against the will of God.

"In either case, I shall raise no hand! Wouldn't I look a little strange trying to stay in control if God desires that I fall?"

"But you know that Absalom should not be king!" replied Abishai in frustration.

"Do I? No man knows. Only God knows, and he has not spoken. I did not fight to be king, and I will not fight to remain king. May God come tonight and take the throne, the kingship, and . . ." David's voice faltered. "And his *anointing* from me. I seek his will, not his power. I repeat, I desire his will more than I desire a position of leadership. He may be through with me."

"King David?" A voice came from behind the two men.

"Yes? Oh, a messenger. What is it?"

"Absalom. He wishes to see you a moment. He wants to ask permission to go to Hebron to make a sacrifice."

"David," said Abishai hoarsely, "you know what that really means, don't you?"

"Yes, I do."

David turned to the messenger. "Tell Absalom I will be there in a moment."

David looked one last time at the quiet city below, then turned and walked toward the door.

"*Will* you let him go to Hebron?" Abishai demanded.

"I will," said the great king. "Yes, I will."

Then he turned to the messenger. "This is a dark hour for me. When I have finished speaking to Absalom, I shall retire. Tomorrow have one of the prophets come to me for consultation. Or a scribe. On second thought, send me Zadok, the high priest. Ask him to join me here after the evening sacrifice."

Abishai called out once more, softly this time. Admiration flashed across his face. "Good King, thank you."

"For what?" the puzzled king asked as he turned back in the doorway.

"Not for what you have done, but for what you have *not* done. Thank you for not throwing spears, for not rebelling against kings, for not exposing a man in authority when he was so very vulnerable, for not dividing a kingdom, for not attacking young Absaloms who look like young Davids but are not."

He paused. "And thank you for suffering, for being willing to lose everything. Thank you for giving God a free hand to end, and even destroy, your kingdom— if it pleases him. Thank you for being an example to us all.

"And most of all," he chuckled, "thank you for not consulting witches."

Chapter 24

"NATHAN!"

"Yes? Oh, it's you, Zadok."

"You will pardon my intrusion, Nathan, but I have been observing you for several moments now. You were about to enter the throne room, I believe, to see King David?"

"Yes, Zadok. That was my intent, but I have thought better of it. The king has no need of me."

"I am disappointed, Nathan. In my judgment the king has great need of you. He is facing the gravest test of his life. I am not sure he can pass a test as demanding as this one."

"He has *already* passed this test, Zadok," countered Nathan with a sureness in his voice that showed him to be a prophet of God.

"David has already passed this test? Forgive me, Nathan, but I have no idea what you mean. This crisis, as you well know, has just begun."

"Zadok, your king passed *this* test long ago, when he was a young man."

"You speak of Saul? But that, my friend, was a wholly different matter."

"Not at all. It is *exactly* the same. There is really no difference at all. As David related to his God and to the man over him at that time long ago . . . so now David will also relate to his God and to the man under him. There can be no difference. Not ever.

"True, circumstances may be altered . . . slightly. Ever so slightly, I might add. But the heart! Ah, the heart is always the same.

"Zadok, I have always been grateful Saul was our *first* king. I shudder to think of the trouble he might have caused if, as a young man, he had found himself under some other king. There is no real difference between the man who discovers a Saul in his life and the man who finds an Absalom in his life. In either situation, the corrupt heart will find its 'justification.' The Sauls of this world can never see a David; they see only Absalom. The Absaloms of this world can never see a David; they see only Saul."

"And the pure heart?" asked Zadok.

"Ah, now there is a rare thing indeed. How does a man with

a broken heart handle an Absalom? The way he handled a Saul? We will soon know, Zadok!"

"You and I were not privileged to be there when David came to his hour with Saul. But we are privileged to be present in his hour with Absalom. I for one intend to watch this unfolding drama very closely. And in so doing, I have the good expectation of learning a lesson or two. Mark my words, David will work his way through this thing—and he will pass this test with the same grace he displayed in his youth."

"And Absalom?"

"What of Absalom?"

"In a few hours he may be our king. Is that not your point?"

"There is that possibility," replied Zadok, almost with humor.

Nathan laughed. "If Absalom gains the throne, may heaven have mercy on all the Sauls, Davids, *and* Absaloms of the realm!

"In my judgment our young Absalom will make a splendid Saul," continued Nathan as he turned and strolled down the long corridor.

"Yes. A splendid Saul. For in every way but age and position, Absalom is already a Saul."

Chapter 25

"I THANK YOU FOR COMING, ZADOK."

"My king."

"You are a priest of God. Could you tell me a story of long ago?"

"What story, my king?"

"Do you know the story of Moses?"

"I do."

"Tell it to me."

"It is long; shall I tell it all?"

"No, not all."

"Then what part?"

"Tell me about Korah's rebellion."

The high priest stared at David with eyes burning. David stared back, his also ablaze. The two men understood.

"I shall tell you the story of Korah's rebellion and of Moses' behavior in the midst of that rebellion.

"Many have heard the story of Moses. He is the supreme example of the Lord's anointed. God's true government rests upon a man—no, upon the contrite heart of a man. There is no form or order to God's government; there is only a man or woman with a contrite heart. Moses was such a man.

"Korah was not such a man, although he was the first cousin of Moses. Korah wanted the authority Moses had. One peaceful morning, Korah awoke. There was no discord among God's people that morning, but before the day was over he had found 252 men to agree with his charges against Moses."

"Then there were problems in the nation when Moses ruled?" asked David.

"There are always problems in any kingdom," replied Zadok. "Always. Furthermore, the ability to be able to see those problems is a cheap gift, indeed."

David smiled and asked, "But, Zadok, you know there have been unjust kingdoms and unjust rulers and pretenders and liars who have ruled and governed. How can a simple people know which is a kingdom with faults but led by men of God, and which is a kingdom unworthy of men's submission? How can a people know?"

David stopped; he realized that he had hit upon what he wished most of all to know. Heavily, he spoke again. "And the king—how can he know? Can he know if he is just? Can he know if the charges are of great worth? Are there signs?" David's final words were anxious.

"Are you looking for some list let down from heaven, David? Even if there were such a list, even if there were a way to know, wicked men would arrange their kingdoms to fit the list! And if such a list existed and a good man filled it to perfection, there would be rebels claiming he had not fulfilled one qualification listed therein. You underestimate the human heart, David."

"Then how shall the people know?"

"They cannot know."

"You mean that in the midst of a hundred voices making a thousand claims, the simple people of God have no assurance of who is truly anointed to bear God's authority and who is not?"

"They can never be certain."

"Who, then, can know?"

"God always knows—but he does not tell."

"Is there no hope, then, for those who must follow unworthy men?"

"Their grandchildren will be able to see the matter clearly. *They* will know. But those caught up in the drama? They can never be certain. Nonetheless, a good thing will come from it all."

"What is that?"

"As surely as the sun rises, people's hearts will be tested. Despite the many claims—and counterclaims—the hidden motives within the hearts of all who are involved will be revealed. This might not seem important in the eyes of men, but in the eyes of God such things are central. The motives of the heart will eventually be revealed. God will see to it."

"I despise such tests," replied David wearily. "I hate such nights as this one. Yet God seems to send many, many things into my life to test this heart of mine. Once more, this night, I find my heart on trial.

"Zadok, there is something that bothers me above all else. Perhaps God *is* finished with me. Is there not some way for me to know?"

"I know of no other ruler in all history who would even ask the question, Good King. Most other men would have ripped their opponent—or even their imagined opponent—to shreds by now. But to answer your questions, I know of no way for you to be certain that God is—or is not—finished with you."

David sighed and choked back a sob. "Then continue with the story. Korah had 252 followers, did he? What happened next?"

"Korah approached Moses and Aaron with his followers. He informed Moses that he had no right to all the authority he exercised."

"Well, we Hebrews are consistent, aren't we?" laughed David.

"No, the heart of man is consistent, David," replied Zadok.

"Tell me, what was Moses' response to Korah?"

"At the age of forty, Moses had been an arrogant, self-willed man, not unlike Korah. What he might have done at forty, I cannot say. At eighty, he was a broken man. He was . . ."

"The meekest man who ever lived," interrupted David.

"The man who carries the rod of God's authority should be. Otherwise God's people will live in terror. Yes, a broken man faced Korah. And I believe you already know what Moses did, David. He did . . . nothing."

"Nothing. Ah, what a man."

"He fell on his face before God. That is all he did."

"Why did he do that, Zadok?"

"David, you of all men must know. Moses knew that God alone had put him in charge of Israel. There was nothing that needed to be done. Korah and his 252 followers would seize the kingdom—or God would vindicate Moses. Moses knew that."

"Men would find it hard to imitate such a life, would they not? An imposter surely could not fake such surrender, could he? But tell me, how did God vindicate Moses?"

"Moses told the men to return the next day with censers and incense . . . and God would decide the issue."

"So!" cried David. "So!" he exclaimed again even louder. "Sometimes God *does* tell," he said excitedly. "Please continue."

"Korah and two of his friends were swallowed by the earth. The other 250 died by . . ."

"Never mind," said David. "Suffice it to say that Moses was proven to be in authority . . . by God! God *did* tell! The people knew who really had authority from God, and at last Moses had rest."

"No, David. He did not find rest, and the people were not satisfied with God's answer! The very next day the whole congregation murmured against Moses, and they would all have died except for the prayers of Moses."

"And men fight to become kings!" David shook his head in perplexity.

Zadok paused, then continued: "David, I perceive that you are torn by the question of what is true authority and what is not. You want to know what to do with a rebellion, if indeed it is a rebellion and not the hand of God. I trust you will find the only pure thing to do—and do it. And thereby you will teach us all."

The door opened, and Abishai rushed in. "Good King! Your son, your own flesh and blood, has proclaimed himself *king* in Hebron. At first impression, it seems all Israel has gone over to him. He plans to take the throne. He marches toward Jerusalem. Some of the men closest to you have gone over to him."

David walked away. He spoke quietly to himself. "Israel's third king? Do true leaders of the kingdom of God gain authority in this way?"

Zadok, not certain if he should be hearing David's words or not, spoke out. "My king?"

David turned, his eyes moist.

"At last," David said quietly. "At last this matter will be resolved. Perhaps tomorrow someone besides God will know."

"Perhaps," said Zadok, "but perhaps not. Such questions may be debated even after we are all dead."

"That might also be tomorrow," laughed David. "Go, Abishai, tell Joab. You will find him in the turret of the east wall."

Abishai departed as he had entered, in haste and in fury.

"I wonder, Zadok," mused David, "if a man can force God into a position where he *must* tell."

Chapter 26

ABISHAI RUSHED ACROSS THE COURTYARD and into the eastern rampart, where he charged up the spiral staircase. At the top of the stairs, Joab stared down at Abishai. In the flickering light of torches, each man studied the face of the other.

Abishai spoke. "Have you heard, Joab?"

"Have I heard! 'Tis midnight, yet half the city is awake with the word. How can it be, Abishai—a son against his own father!"

"When kingdoms are vulnerable, men see queer sights," responded Abishai with a distant stare.

"And they'll sacrifice anything to satisfy ambition," added Joab angrily. "What think you of these things, Abishai?"

"What think I?" responded Abishai, matching Joab's anger with his own rage. "This! Absalom has no authority in the kingdom. He holds no power, no office, yet he has risen up to divide the kingdom. He has raised his hand against the very anointed of God—against David! David—who has never done or spoken one evil word against him.

"What think I?" Abishai's voice rose toward a crescendo. "If Absalom, who has no authority, will commit this deed; if Absalom, who is nothing, will divide the very kingdom of God—" His voice now rolled like thunder. "If Absalom will do these evil things *now*, what in the name of sanity might that man do if he be *king?*"

Chapter 27

David and Zadok were alone once more.

"And now, what will you do, David? In your youth, you spoke no word against an unworthy king. What will you do now with an equally unworthy youth?"

"As I said," replied David, "these are the times I hate the most, Zadok. Nonetheless, against all reason, I judge my own heart first and rule against its interests. I will do what I did under Saul. I will leave the destiny of the kingdom in God's hands alone. Perhaps he is finished with me. Perhaps I have sinned too greatly and am no longer worthy to lead. Only God knows if that is true, and it seems he will not tell."

Then, clenching his fist, yet with a touch of wry humor in his voice, David added emphatically, "But today I shall give ample space for this untelling God of ours to show us his will. I know of no other way to bring about such an extraordinary event except by doing *nothing*! The throne is not mine. Not to have, not to take, not to protect, and not to keep.

"I will leave the city. The throne is the Lord's. So is the kingdom. I will not hinder God. No obstacle, no activity on my part lies between me and God's will. Nothing will prevent him from accomplishing his will. If I am not to be king, God will find no difficulty in making Absalom to be Israel's king. Now it is possible. God shall be God!"

The true king turned and walked quietly out of the throne room, out of the palace, out of the city. He walked and he walked . . .

Into the bosoms of all men whose hearts are pure.

Well, dear reader, the time has come for us to say good-bye once more. I will leave you to your thoughts and to reflect on the hidden motives of your own heart.

Oh, by the way, the players are working on a love story. Perhaps we can see it together when it is performed. I believe it shall be called . . . The Divine Romance.

I trust, then, by the mercy of God, we shall meet again.

Book Discussion Guide

1. How can you break the cycle of wounding? What makes this hard to accomplish?

2. God's prophet had anointed David when he was a boy, but for years David saw only hardship and danger. How can a person remain faithful between the promise and the payoff? What might make it difficult to remain faithful even after the payoff has arrived?

3. Have you been broken? Why do we tend to avoid this? Is it always necessary? Are you willing to live through pain, or do you avoid it? When do you most clearly see the sufficiency of God's grace?

4. Who throws spears at you? How does God want you to respond?

5. Are you clinging to God's promises or to God himself? What is the distinction (if any)?

6. Chapter 6 deals largely with God's divine establishment of authority. Read Romans 13 and consider your reaction to these concepts. What do you find hard to swallow? Are there any exceptions to this general rule?

7. Do you agree with the author's assertion that God knows, but he never tells us? How does your answer affect your view of God's relationship with his children?

8. What needs to happen to put your own inner Saul to death?

9. David's men saw the opportunity as a sign from God, but David refused to harm Saul. If an opportunity arose, would you do something drastic to ensure your own safety? to exact justice? to take revenge?

10. The author points out that God does not rescind his gifts, even when people use them unfaithfully. (But contrast the story of Samson in Judges 16.) What does this show about God's character?

11. Do you know any Davids who have been condemned as Sauls?

12. What makes a true leader? How should a real leader approach and handle his or her authority?

13. The author equates rebellion with thievery, taking what is not rightfully one's own. Do you agree with the author's statement that "no rebellion in the Kingdom of God is proper" (p. 64)? What differentiates dissenters or reformers from schismatics and dividers? How would you apply these truths to historical events like the Protestant Reformation or the American Revolution?

14. Do you agree with David's commitment to "raise no hand," or do you find this course too passive? How can we know when God wants us to take action and when he wants us to accept action taken against us?

15. In this story, David considered the throne to be God's, not his own to have, to take, to protect, to keep. He asserted that he desired God's will more than God's blessing (see p. 75). Could you say the same about what God has given you? How would you respond if your job, your home, your family were all taken from you?

16. Sauls see only Absaloms; Absaloms see only Sauls. Neither can recognize a David. How can we distinguish one from the others? Is it true that we can never be certain whether a leader is a Saul or a David, that only God can truly know?

17. The person who wields the rod of God's authority should be the meekest, a broken man, lest his people live in terror. What kind of authority does a true leader have? How should he or she respond to that commission? How should his or her followers respond to that individual?

Please turn the page for an excerpt from
The Prisoner in the Third Cell . . .

Chapter 6

PEOPLE CAME TO HEAR JOHN because they were seeking something to fill a deep vacancy in their lives.

Merchants came to hear him and repented of their business practices, and were then baptized in the fabled waters of the Jordan. Soldiers came, repented of their brutality, and were baptized. The camel drivers came, the farmers, the rustic fishermen, housewives, women of renown, women of the streets, all kinds and all classes came. And all who came, it seemed, came holding some secret sin, repented thereof, and disappeared beneath the Jordan waters.

Every Jew knew the ancient meaning of a soul's being plunged beneath the water of that particular river. It meant the end of life, the cessation of everything. Everyone awaiting baptism stood on the eastern bank, which was a foreign land. There they stepped into the water and disappeared . . . there to die. But each came up out of the water and stepped onto the western bank, safe within the border of the Promised Land, there to begin a new life with God. This simple drama was unforgettable.

There was one particular day at the Jordan that stood out from all others. It began with the arrival of horse-drawn carriages. A delegation of dignitaries had arrived. What important personages had come out to this obscure place?

It was the nation's religious leaders.

When John saw these costumed men, every muscle in his body became motionless. There was not one outer movement on his countenance to betray his inward feelings. As these religious dignitaries cut through the crowd, John watched as ordinary people dropped their heads or genuflected in a gesture of honor. This did not at all set well with the greatest nonconformist of all time.

John read every man as he stepped out of the carriages. Some had obviously come to sneer, to gather evidence against John, and to condemn. Others came with a great deal of uncertainty, hoping to discover for themselves whether or not John was a true prophet. There were even a few among them, the youngest, who came truly believing that John was a man of God. These young men hoped the older, more respected leaders might agree with their unspoken opinion. After all, if the older leaders gave their blessing to John, some of the young men knew they would be free to become his disciples.

But John saw more than this. He looked in the heart of every man now making his way through the midst of the crowd, and discerned the ultimate weakness of each one. There was not *one* among them brave enough, on his own, to break with accepted religious traditions.

The crowd continued giving way before these vaunted leaders. The delegation was on its way to the front of the crowd, to take their rightful place of honor. This was more than the desert prophet could ever hope to stomach. The religious system of his day, coming *here*? And daring to impose their abominable practices *here*? How dare they come! How dare they bring their arrogance, contempt, disdain, and pride to *this* place!

John had not come to this earth to compromise, nor to win over such men to the ways of God. After all, these men saw themselves as authorities in God's ways. John would not attempt to do the impossible: He would not call the leaders of the religious system to come out of that system. Yet the presence of these men was perverting the freedom which the baptized ones had gained as they laid aside the systemization of this world.

John, therefore, declared war. Open, unbridled, unquartered war . . . on Israel's most revered personages. He wanted every human being present to know how he felt about the chains which traditionalists had forged upon the hearts and souls of God's people. And just how did he feel? He felt this whole religious culture must perish.

There was nothing John could do better than thunder, and on this occasion he roared like a lion. Thrusting out the forefinger of one hand, he shattered earth and heaven with his denunciation.

"Who . . . who, I ask . . . who told you to repent?
You nest of snakes, what are you doing here?"

The crowd was stunned. No one had *ever* talked this way to *these* men. Many in the crowd instinctively rose to their feet; after a moment, wide grins began to appear on the faces of some. But every eye was now riveted on the religious leaders. What would be their reaction? And, was it possible . . . had John committed some kind of blasphemy? The people knew the rumors about John being possessed of a demon; this was not going to help. They loved him for his boldness, yet no one ever dreamed he would take on the religious leaders of their nation. *No one* did that!

Shock turned to disbelief as John continued.

"I ask you again, you nest of snakes, who told you to turn
away from the wrath that is coming on you?"

The religious leaders stopped. No one could speak to them in this way. After a brief moment, one of the leaders pulled his cloak up about him, turned and whispered something to those nearest him. They, in turn, signaled to the others to make a sudden retreat.

But John was not finished.

"Your tree! An axe has been laid to your tree. The wrath of God is upon you. The axe will cut down your tree and destroy its root. The day is not far when all that you are shall be destroyed under the wrath of God."

With that the delegation, as one, gathered up their outer robes and hurried back toward their carriages, each devising in his heart some form of vengeance to take against John.

Someone in the crowd began to cheer. Someone else clapped. With that, the whole multitude stood and took up the applause. Everywhere men and women felt shackles falling from their souls. At last, someone had dared to challenge the religious system!

Spontaneously, the multitude moved toward John. It seemed that every soul present who had not been baptized wanted very much to do so now. They had all, as one, glimpsed something deeper of John's message, something they had never understood before.

It was a glorious day. Yet no one seemed to have laid hold of the obvious. Conduct like this would get John killed.

And then there was that other very memorable day.

Chapter 7

THE DOOR FROM THE OTHER realm opened, like a window, just over the Jordan River. Out from the very center of the being of God the Father came forth His own sacred Spirit, the Holy Spirit, somewhat as a dove might, fluttering out through the open door and coming to rest on one of the spectators who was listening to John speak.

John's eyes scanned the crowed, his fierce gaze catching every face. What was that? A light of unnatural origin, appearing out of nowhere, like a dove flying out of a window and coming to rest on someone out there in the crowd.

John realized he was seeing what no other eye could see. This was the sign of the Messiah. John fell silent. His only thought was, "Where landed the lighted dove? *Who* is out there?"

Murmuring whispers swept across the crowd. Many followed John's searching gaze.

Spontaneously, John roared

"Behold the Lamb of God!

"I am nothing. This man is everything. Look no more to me, look to *him.* As for me, I am not even worthy to stoop down and unlatch the sandals that are on the feet of this one."

The Father seemed to agree. Standing in the door between the two realms, He called out.

"This is my beloved Son in whom I am well pleased."

And as God was pleased, so John was pleased. Nor did it bother John as he watched the multitudes forsake him and begin to follow Jesus. After all, John knew he had come into the world for this very reason.

What John did not know was that the easiest days of his work were now behind him. The harder were yet to come.

GENE EDWARDS was born and raised in east Texas, the son of an oil-field roughneck. He was converted to Christ in his junior year in college. He graduated from East Texas State University in Commerce, Texas, at the age of eighteen, with majors in English literature and history. His first year of postgraduate work was taken at the Baptist Theological Seminary in Rüschlikon, Switzerland. He received his master's degree in theology from Southwestern Baptist Theological Seminary in Ft. Worth, Texas at the age of twenty-two. He served as a Southern Baptist pastor and then as an evangelist for ten years.

Today his ministry includes conferences on the deeper Christian life and on living that life in the context of a practical experience of church life. There have been seventy translations of his books in eighteen languages.

Gene and his wife, Helen, now make their home in Jacksonville, Florida. The author can be reached at the following address:

Gene Edwards
P. O. Box 3450
Jacksonville, FL 32206
www.geneedwards.com

A Tale of Three Kings and its sequel, *The Prisoner in the Third Cell*, have become modern Christian classics, and readers everywhere have acclaimed *The Divine Romance* as one of the finest pieces of Christian literature of our time and a magnificent saga that will take your breath away. Here is an incomparable love story told in almost childlike simplicity, yet revealing some of the deepest truths of the Christian faith.

Also in the same genre is the spellbinding story of the history of God's people . . . as seen by the angels—The Chronicles of Heaven series (*The Beginning, The Escape, The Birth, The Triumph, The Return*). In addition, The First-Century Diaries series presents the sweeping panorama of the entire saga of the first-century church.

Gene Edwards has written three books that serve as an introduction to the deeper Christian life: *Living by the Highest Life, The Secret to the Christian Life*, and *The Inward Journey*. For a complete list of books by Gene Edwards, see the page opposite the title page.

Three modern classics by Gene Edwards

A tyrant, a usurper, a willing vessel.

"You cannot tell who is the Lord's anointed and who is not."

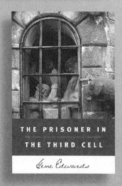

A man of God imprisoned in the darkest of places: his own doubts.

"Will you follow a God who does not live up to your expectations?"

The greatest love story ever told.

"Turn back, O City. Turn back, O bride of God."